POSITIVE AFFIRMATIONS AND ACTIONS FOR BUILDING YOUR
Side Hustle

PRACTICE POSITIVITY AND BUILD AN
ENTREPRENEUR'S MINDSET WITH
DAILY RITUALS AND MANIFESTING

Published by Turtle Publishing
All rights reserved.

Printed on demand in Australia, United States and United Kingdom.

Written & designed by Kathy Shanks
© Kathy Shanks 2021
Illustrations by Freepik Storyset & Turtle Publishing

No part of this publication may be reproduced, stored in a retrieval system, or transmitted in any form or by any means, electronic, mechanical, photocopying, recording or otherwise, without the prior written permission of the author.

Under no circumstances will any blame or legal responsibility be held against the publisher, or author, for any damages, reparation, or monetary loss due to the information contained within this book including, but not limited to — errors, omissions, or inaccuracies. Either directly or indirectly. You are responsible for your own choices, actions, and results.

Legal Notice: This book is copyright protected. This book is only for personal use. You cannot amend, distribute, sell, use, quote or paraphrase any part, or the content within this book, without the consent of the author or publisher.

Disclaimer: Please note the information contained within this document is for educational and entertainment purposes only. All effort has been executed to present accurate, up to date, and reliable, complete information. No warranties of any kind are declared or implied. Readers acknowledge that the author is not engaging in the rendering of legal, financial, medical or professional advice. The content within this book has been derived from various sources. Please consult a licensed professional before attempting any techniques outlined in this book.

SPECIAL BONUS
FREE BOOKS

FREE Workbook to begin an intentional journaling practice.

FREE 30 Days to Greater Self Love Program

Get FREE unlimited access to these AND all of my new books by joining our fan base!

SCAN WITH YOUR CAMERA OR GO TO
bit.ly/AffGifts

How to use this book

On the left-hand pages are affirmations. On the right-hand pages are actions for you to take to strengthen your entrepreneurial mindset.

You may like to work through this book one page per day, or perhaps you'd like to trust divine guidance. Hold this book close to your heart or navel, close your eyes, take three gentle breaths, and as you breathe out on the third breath, open the book. We trust that you will be guided to the page you need the most.

Introduction

When it comes to a career or business, success can look like so many different things to different people. For some, it could mean working your way up the corporate ladder and clinching that top spot. For others, it could mean being able to turn your passion into a lucrative venture. It could even be as broad as achieving financial independence.

No matter what your picture of success is, there's no denying that getting there doesn't happen overnight—it's a journey filled with challenges, setbacks, and, yes, sometimes, even failures.

Navigating that journey demands certain qualities of us. Contemplate the people you consider to have absolutely, unquestionably achieved success. What are they like? How do they think? What do they believe, and how does that manifest in their work?

Regardless of field or industry, you'll find that the most successful people have one thing in common: an entrepreneurial mindset.

In a nutshell, the entrepreneurial mindset is the ability to identify opportunities and take steps to maximise these. This may sound like a tall order, but this is actually underpinned by certain core values and qualities that extend even beyond business and succeeding in your professional life.

First, passion and motivation are key to succeeding as an entrepreneur. Again, the road to your goals won't always be smooth. To get through those tough times, you need that inner fire and drive—persistence and hard work are only possible when these come from a place deep within you.

Creativity is also an important ingredient of the entrepreneurial mindset. Now, this doesn't necessarily mean 'artistic.' Essentially, it's the ability to take existing ideas and insights to come up with something new. Creative thinking comes into play across so many different things, from finding solutions to business challenges, finding more efficient ways to do things, and forging new paths.

Successful people also exhibit a willingness to learn. Any idea—even the best of the best—can always be better, and a great entrepreneur is always open to constructive input from other people. Also, this openness is what will enable you to use mistakes to your advantage; through the lens of learning.

Lastly, and perhaps most importantly, is self-belief. A huge part of being a successful entrepreneur is getting people on board with you—how would you manage to do that if you aren't a hundred per cent on board yourself? How is anybody else supposed to believe in you if you don't? Being confident in the value you offer will inspire the same confidence in others, whether its customers or business partners. Self-belief comes from a strong sense of who you are, where you stand, and what you stand for. Any venture requires a degree of risk at some point—having this foundation makes you unshakeable, or at the very least, resilient.

With everything else on your plate, though, it can be hard to see yourself taking the time out to work on all of these qualities and hone your skills further. But, think of it this way: deliberately working on developing an entrepreneur's mindset is an active investment in yourself and your business.

And, it can be as simple as spending a few minutes on an affirmation practice each day. Being a business owner can pull you in several different directions at any given moment. There is always something to do, a conversation to be had, a decision that has to be made. Affirmations can help you re-centre and go back to what truly matters. These can be powerful tools to stay focused—on your goals, the foundation you are rooting from, and the tools you are sharpening to aid you on your journey.

Especially for self-belief, affirmations can be an amazing way to unlock and cultivate the entrepreneurial mindset. There's a reason it's called an affirmation practice—the very mechanism behind affirmations can be compared to working out or physical training. By repeating positive thought patterns, you reinforce certain connections and functions in your brain. Through time, these become easier to access and tap into.

Success—whatever that may be to you—starts within. You already have everything you need. All that's left to do is plant the seeds with thought, water them with action, and before you know it, you'll be reaping the fruits of your efforts.

"Every time you state what you want or believe, you're the first to hear it. It's a message to both you and others about what you think is possible. Don't put a ceiling on yourself."

- Oprah Winfrey

AFFIRMATIONS

I see every day as an opportunity.

ACTIONS

Write down your biggest, boldest dreams. Don't be afraid to get as specific and detailed as you want!

AFFIRMATIONS

I am capable of great things.

ACTIONS

Commit to learning something new, whether it's a skill, a hobby, or even just an interesting new concept or fact.

AFFIRMATIONS

I am on an amazing journey towards my goals.

ACTIONS

Think of someone you look up to—perhaps a leader in your field, or someone whose success you aspire for—and try to list down the qualities you admire in them.

AFFIRMATIONS

Every day takes me closer to my goals.

ACTIONS

Create a vision board and display it somewhere you can always see.

AFFIRMATIONS

I am skilled, intelligent, and competent.

ACTIONS

Do at least one thing every day that counts towards your goals.

AFFIRMATIONS

I surround myself with people who share my drive and values.

ACTIONS

Take a long walk while listening to a podcast that interests or inspires you.

AFFIRMATIONS

I am worthy
of the success
I envision for
myself.

ACTIONS

Clear the clutter from your physical or digital workspace.

AFFIRMATIONS

I believe in my abilities and power to succeed.

ACTIONS

Write down what success means to you. What does it look like? What does it feel like?

AFFIRMATIONS

I am filled with boundless potential.

ACTIONS

List down 5 skills or abilities you are proud to have.

AFFIRMATIONS

There are no limits to what I am capable of.

ACTIONS

Celebrate even little wins—it can be as simple as treating yourself to a scoop of ice cream for getting through a long workday.

AFFIRMATIONS

I have what
it takes to
overcome any
challenge that
comes my way.

ACTIONS

Think about the toughest challenge you've taken on at work. How did you overcome it, and how did you feel afterwards?

AFFIRMATIONS

I am great at channelling positive energy into action.

ACTIONS

Put on some upbeat, energising music to kick-start your workday!

AFFIRMATIONS

I trust my own judgment.

ACTIONS

Challenge yourself to try something you've always wanted to do but have been too afraid to.

AFFIRMATIONS

I have the ability to make good decisions.

ACTIONS

Put together a daily or weekly checklist of small-yet-impactful, realistic, and achievable wins. Don't forget to tick items off as you go along!

AFFIRMATIONS

I am focused
and motivated.

ACTIONS

Dress for success, whatever it means to you. It doesn't necessarily have to mean 'fancy'—as long as it makes you feel confident and in control, you're all set.

AFFIRMATIONS

I am supported by people who care about me and want me to achieve my goals.

ACTIONS

Even during the busiest of days, don't forget to take breaks. Even just for 10 minutes a time, allow yourself to step away from work and rest or do something completely unrelated.

AFFIRMATIONS

I am inspired
and empowered
in my journey
towards
success.

ACTIONS

When faced with a tough situation that requires a decision or response, always take a moment to absorb and reflect before moving into action.

AFFIRMATIONS

Abundance flows naturally to me.

ACTIONS

Be someone's accountability partner and have them be yours. Check-in with each other regularly to share updates on your progress towards your respective goals.

AFFIRMATIONS

I have all the tools that I need to make my dreams a reality.

ACTIONS

Take a negative thought, comment, or situation and challenge yourself to turn it into something positive.

AFFIRMATIONS

Everything that I need to succeed is already within me.

ACTIONS

Make it a daily habit to read a few pages—or better yet, a whole chapter—of any book of your choice.

AFFIRMATIONS

I am passionate about my dreams.

ACTIONS

Choose one of your biggest goals and create a 90-day action plan for it. This doesn't necessarily mean you have to reach the goal itself in 90 days—you simply have to take significant strides towards it.

AFFIRMATIONS

I am in a prime position to prosper.

ACTIONS

Close your eyes and imagine the future you want for yourself. Really try to picture where you'll be, what you'll be doing, and even the things you'll have.

AFFIRMATIONS

Money flows
to me in
abundance.

ACTIONS

Join social groups that share your passions and give yourself opportunities to engage with equally ambitious and motivated people.

AFFIRMATIONS

I am deserving of the wealth I desire.

ACTIONS

Reach out to and connect with people you can learn from—you can even look into tapping mentors or coaches for your specific goals.

AFFIRMATIONS

I am always eager to learn and discover new things.

ACTIONS

Make it a habit to jot down your random thoughts, ideas, and questions—you never know what future potential these may hold.

AFFIRMATIONS

I am not afraid to ask questions.

ACTIONS

Shake things up with a change in scenery—try taking your work outdoors or, at the very least, to a different spot in your house.

AFFIRMATIONS

I am open to diverse ideas.

ACTIONS

When spending long hours working seated, make sure to get up and move around every once in a while. Take a couple of minutes to stretch out your arms, legs, neck and back.

AFFIRMATIONS

I am someone the best of the best would like to work with.

ACTIONS

Strike up a conversation with someone you wouldn't usually have the chance to talk to—there's something to learn from everyone.

AFFIRMATIONS

I am in charge
of my life and
my success.

ACTIONS

Visit a local exhibition or museum and just soak everything in.

AFFIRMATIONS

I do not let
stumbling
blocks
discourage me.

ACTIONS

Write about your proudest moment or most significant achievement.

AFFIRMATIONS

I am exactly the kind of leader that I want to be.

ACTIONS

What's something you can do today that will make you feel like the person you aspire to be 5 years from now? Do it.

AFFIRMATIONS

I am an overflowing spring of great ideas.

ACTIONS

Spend an afternoon immersed in a creative activity you enjoy without worrying about the output.

AFFIRMATIONS

I am a bold, creative, innovative thinker.

ACTIONS

Update your resume and get your professional profile or portfolio in order.

AFFIRMATIONS

I welcome growth and positive change.

ACTIONS

Include setting an intention for the day in your morning ritual.

AFFIRMATIONS

I release self-doubt.

ACTIONS

Wrap up your workday by jotting down a quick to-do list that will help you hit the ground running on the following day.

AFFIRMATIONS

I open
myself up to
opportunities
and abundance.

ACTIONS

Try to never hit the snooze button.

AFFIRMATIONS

I am confident
in my abilities.

ACTIONS

Write about a moment when you felt on top of the world—confident, in control, and amazing.

AFFIRMATIONS

I am steadfast in my determination to reach my goals.

ACTIONS

Learn a new language! No need to worry about mastering it or even becoming conversational—
just go at your own pace and enjoy the process.

AFFIRMATIONS

I define and
shape my
own picture of
success.

ACTIONS

Define your support system. List down people you can count on, with the specific things you know they can help you with.

AFFIRMATIONS

I am adaptable and resilient.

ACTIONS

Read an inspirational biography or autobiography.

AFFIRMATIONS

I can handle whatever challenges come my way.

ACTIONS

Write about the word 'confidence.' What does it mean to you? How does it feel? What are some ways you can cultivate it in yourself?

AFFIRMATIONS

I don't need everything to go my way to succeed.

ACTIONS

Get your budget and finances in order and commit to tracking these religiously.

AFFIRMATIONS

I've got all the
smarts and
savvy I need.

ACTIONS

Declutter your inbox.

AFFIRMATIONS

I put my heart into everything I do.

ACTIONS

What's your favourite inspirational or motivational quote? Write it down and consider using it as your desktop or phone wallpaper.

AFFIRMATIONS

My best is enough.

ACTIONS

When discussing ideas at work or brainstorming with your team, practice saying "Yes, and…" instead of "No."

AFFIRMATIONS

I know when and how to ask for help when I need it.

ACTIONS

Challenge yourself to overcome mental barriers. What would you be doing if failure weren't a possibility?

AFFIRMATIONS

I actively learn from others who know more than I do.

ACTIONS

List down 10 things you want to learn.

AFFIRMATIONS

I will succeed without compromising my values and beliefs.

ACTIONS

Find ways to share your passions with others. Is there anyone interested in learning from or being mentored by you? Reach out to them.

AFFIRMATIONS

I am willing to put in the work to make my dreams come true.

ACTIONS

List down 5 things you've done this week that have brought you closer to your goals.

AFFIRMATIONS

I am unstoppable in pursuit of my goals.

ACTIONS

What's one difficult conversation you've been putting off? Can you work towards finally having it soon?

AFFIRMATIONS

I am not afraid to try.

ACTIONS

Be vocal about your goals—tell someone close to you all about what you're aiming to achieve and how you're planning to get there.

AFFIRMATIONS

As long as I do my best, everything will turn out as it should.

ACTIONS

Write down one thing you are struggling with, and 5 things you are doing (or plan to do) to overcome it.

AFFIRMATIONS

I release any worry or anxiety about the future.

ACTIONS

If possible, find ways to arrange your schedule in a manner that honours whether you're a morning or night person.

AFFIRMATIONS

I am the author
of my life story.

ACTIONS

Get out of your comfort zone and attend an industry event where you can expand your professional network.

AFFIRMATIONS

I am not defined by past mistakes.

ACTIONS

Describe what you think the experience is or would be like for someone who works for you.

AFFIRMATIONS

I am capable of turning roadblocks into stepping-stones.

ACTIONS

Do some research on quick tips and lifehacks that are relevant to your field or business.

AFFIRMATIONS

There is nothing
standing in
the way of my
success.

ACTIONS

Volunteer for a career day talk at a local school.

AFFIRMATIONS

I will not allow my spark to be dimmed.

ACTIONS

Write about how you are making the world a better place in your own way.

AFFIRMATIONS

My vision of the future is clear and vivid.

ACTIONS

Think back to your childhood. What did you want to be when you grew up? Write about why that was your dream.

AFFIRMATIONS

I am right where I need to be at this point in my life.

ACTIONS

Ask someone you consider successful for one piece of career or life advice.

AFFIRMATIONS

I will show up
for myself and
for my dreams.

ACTIONS

Set up a system of tracking your goals. It could be a journal, an app, or even just a spreadsheet—don't worry if it takes some trial and error to find what works for you.

AFFIRMATIONS

I am clearing
the path
towards wealth
and success.

ACTIONS

Even when they're different from the consensus, practice speaking up and voicing your opinions politely but firmly.

AFFIRMATIONS

I bring my own unique perspective to the table.

ACTIONS

Draw out a word cloud or mind map with 'success' as the centre.

AFFIRMATIONS

I am a valued asset to those I work with.

ACTIONS

What do you usually spend most of your time on? How about the least time? As an experiment, track your time for a day and see what you can learn from the exercise.

AFFIRMATIONS

I do not shy
away from my
own greatness.

ACTIONS

What do you consider your core values? Write them down, and from your list, try to create a personal mantra.

AFFIRMATIONS

I stand in the
light unafraid.

ACTIONS

Look into any certifications relevant to your field and consider working towards one.

AFFIRMATIONS

Every day, I only get better and better at what I do.

ACTIONS

List down 5 of your worst work and productivity habits. What steps can you take to break them?

AFFIRMATIONS

I continuously hone my craft and sharpen my skills.

ACTIONS

Define your 'why.' List down the people and things that motivate you and keep you going in your journey towards success.

AFFIRMATIONS

I am brimming with joyful anticipation for what I am yet to achieve.

ACTIONS

Train yourself to respond with "I'll try" every time you're tempted to think or say "I can't".

AFFIRMATIONS

My ideas can make a difference in the world.

ACTIONS

Let go of past mistakes by listing down 5 of what you consider your 'failures' or regrets. Then, physically crumple up that piece of paper and throw it away.

AFFIRMATIONS

I stay the course, even when things don't go as planned.

ACTIONS

If you work on a computer, try using a standing desk for a few hours each day.

AFFIRMATIONS

I am built for success.

ACTIONS

List down 5 ways you make your boss', team or client's life easier.

AFFIRMATIONS

I move through life with purpose.

ACTIONS

Find a digital organisation, labelling, and filing system that works for you.

AFFIRMATIONS

I embrace and enjoy every phase of my journey.

ACTIONS

As much as possible, avoid working overtime or allowing work to make its way into personal or family time.

AFFIRMATIONS

My life's best is still to come.

ACTIONS

Although it can be challenging, respond to constructive feedback with an open mind—always starting with "I hear you, thank you," is a great habit to practice.

Also available by **Kathy Shanks**...

Guided Journaling is available worldwide as print or ebook at Amazon, Booktopia, Barnes & Noble and all good bookstores.

Also available in Australia from **turtlepublishing.com.au**

Inside this book you'll discover how to use my method of journaling to:

- Work towards creating balance for heart, mind, body and soul without sacrificing career and relationships
- Create rituals that help you develop gratitude
- Use daily affirmations to practice positivity and manifest your future dreams
- Discover strategies to improve your relationships, build your life mission, start a side hustle, discover yourself, develop self-love, improve your health AND improve your mindset

It seems too good to be true, right! Organising your thoughts and dreams in 10-20 minutes a day can be that one simple change that actually makes your dreams become a reality.

Make your journal your safe haven, a place of nurturing for you to come and reflect, clear your mind, set goals, develop gratitude, make plans, dream, and take steps towards the future that has always seemed just out of reach.

> Please join our journaling community at
> **facebook.com/groups/kathyshanks**
> for exclusive insider access to updates and releases

Also available in the
Guided Journaling Series...

Journaling for a
Balanced Life with a
Health focus

Journaling for a
Balanced Life with a
Life Mission focus

Journaling for a
Balanced Life with a
focus on the **Heart**

Journaling for a
Balanced Life with a
Gratitude & **Manifest** focus

We have a selection of *journals* available worldwide as
print or ebook at Amazon, Booktopia,
Barnes & Noble and all good bookstores.
Also available in Australia from **turtlepublishing.com.au**

www.ingramcontent.com/pod-product-compliance
Lightning Source LLC
Chambersburg PA
CBHW020323010526
44107CB00054B/1954